This book is dedicated to my children, Dylan and Emma. As I embarked on the journey of creating this literary work, my intention was to explore subjects that are often overlooked within the traditional school curriculum, with the aim of nurturing well-rounded and knowledgeable young individuals. Love Aba.

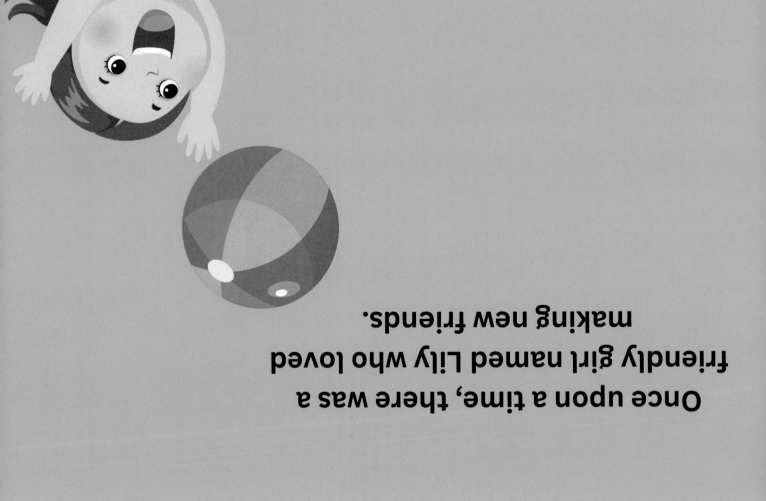

Once upon a time, there was a friendly girl named Lily who loved making new friends.

Lily knew that having good social skills was important for building bridges with others. such as...

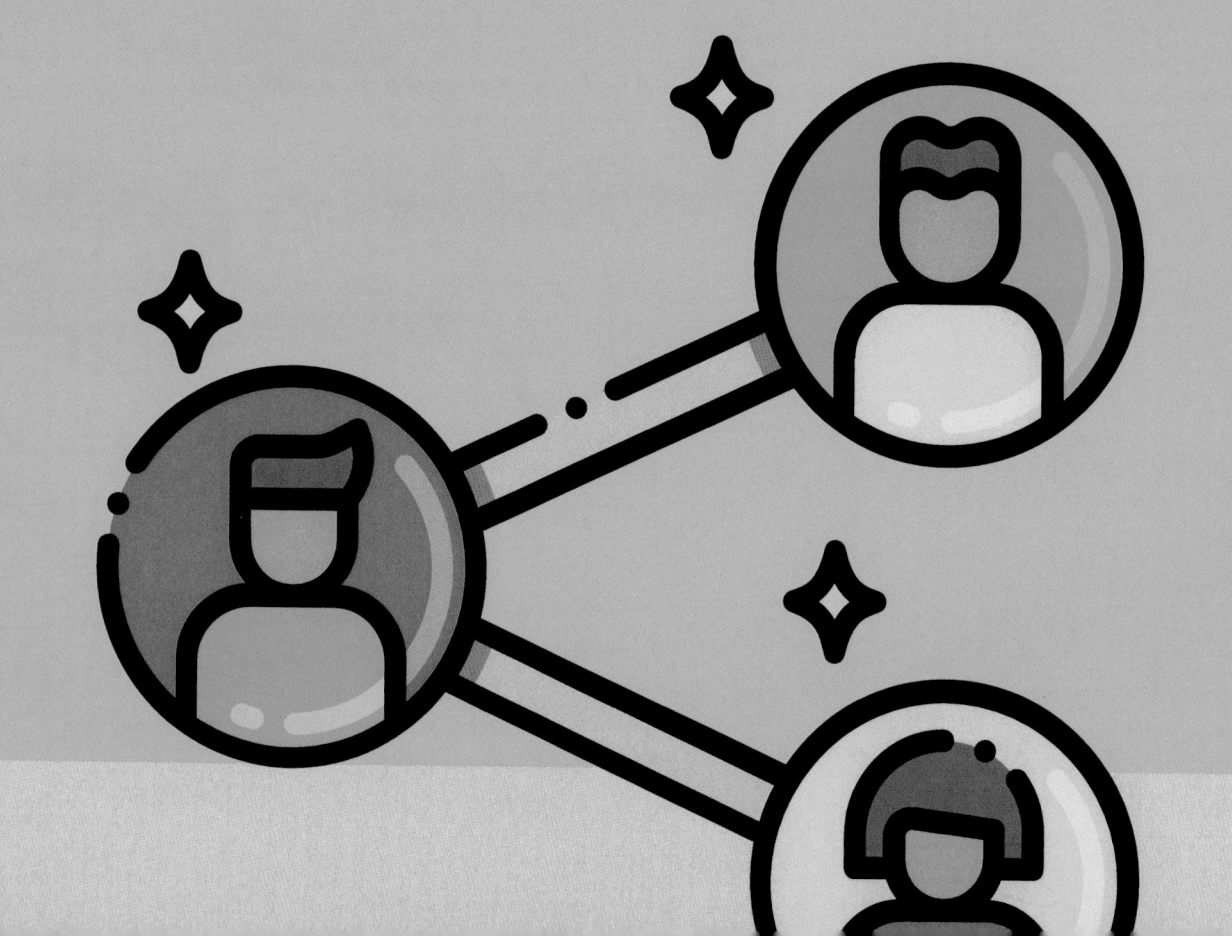

Empathy is the magic key to understanding how others feel.

When Lily saw someone sad, she would lend a helping hand and make them happy.

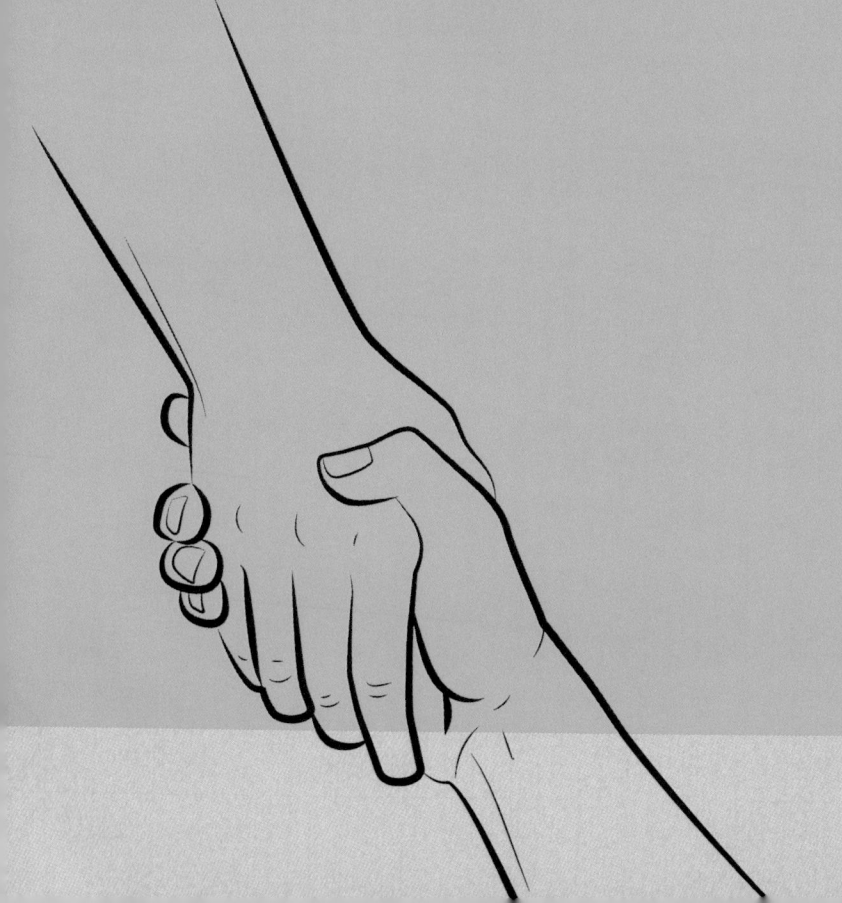

Active listening means giving your full attention, looking into their eyes, and understanding what they say.

Lily learned to listen carefully to her friends, making them feel heard and special.

Effective communication is like painting with words. It helps us express our thoughts and feelings.

Welcome!

THANK YOU!

PLEASE!

Lily __practiced__ using kind words, sharing her ideas, and expressing herself respectfully.

Conflict can sometimes arise, but with problem-solving skills, we can find a compromise and make things right.

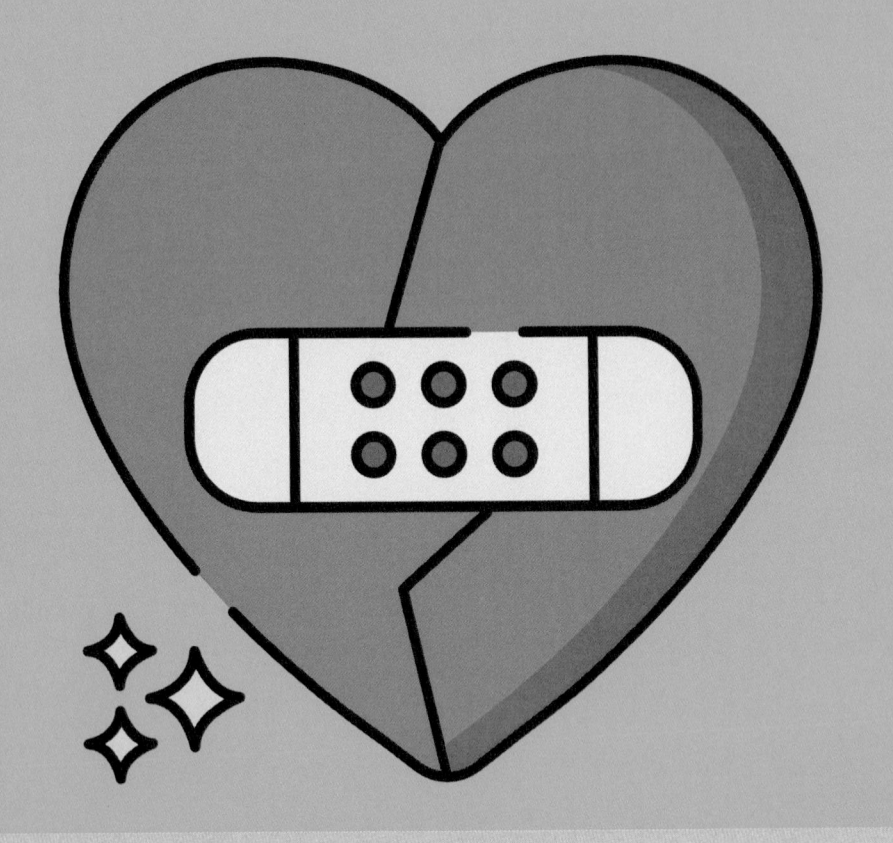

Lily learned to find solutions that make everyone happy, turning frowns into smiles.

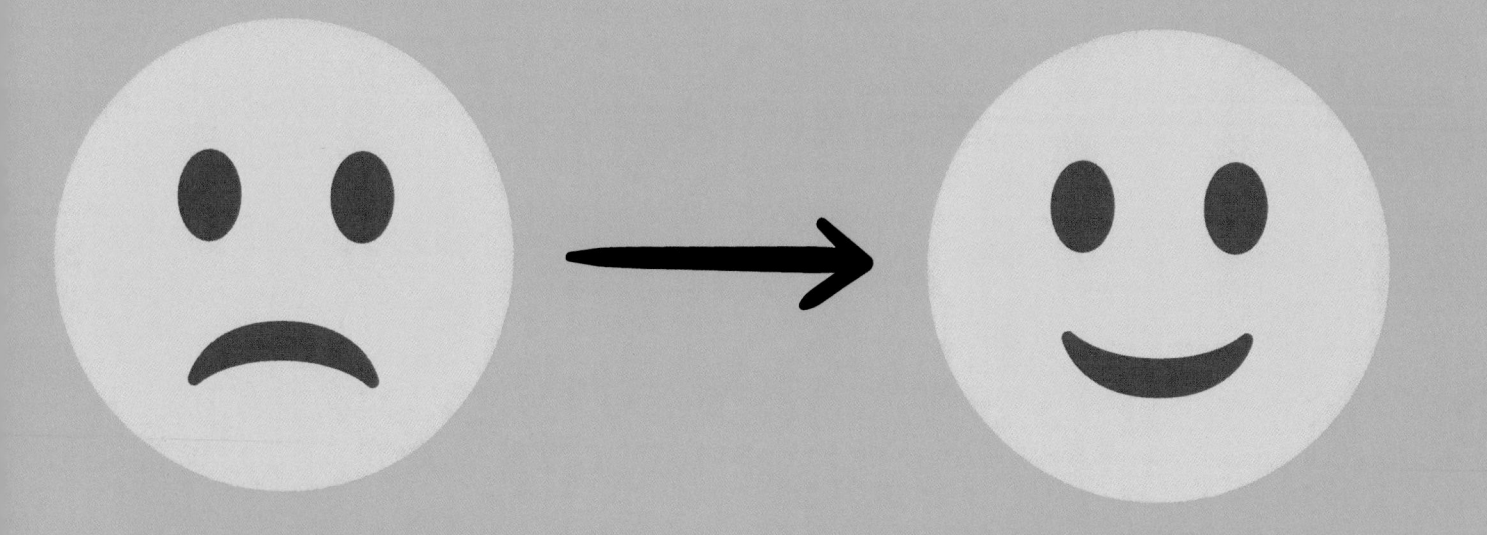

In school, Lily made sure to include everyone, creating a friendly and welcoming environment.

During playtime, Lily encouraged teamwork and cooperation to build bridges of friendship.

At home, Lily helped her family by listening, understanding, and showing empathy.

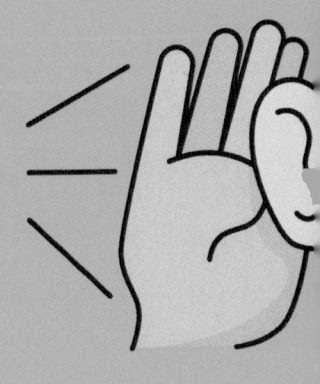

Lily knew that small acts of kindness can make a big difference in someone's day.

Sometimes, making friends might feel scary, but with social skills, Lily made it easy and fun.

Lily discovered that building bridges with others brings joy and happiness to everyone involved.

She loved seeing the smiles on her friend's faces and knowing that she made a positive impact.

No matter how big or small, every bridge she built made the world a better place.

y's social skills grew stronger, and
her friendships blossomed like
beautiful flowers.

The endearing adventures of Lily taught us the
power of social skills and how they can bring us
closer together.

Remember, dear reader, you have
the power to build bridges too!

Be kind, listen, and communicate with love, and
you'll see the magic of social skills all around you.

Now, it's your turn to practice and make new friends wherever you go.

Go forth and build bridges of friendship, just like Lily, the kind-hearted girl.

The world needs your kindness and social skills to make it a better place.

So, spread your wings and soar, for you have the power to build bridges forevermore.

The end.

40127924R00015

BUILDING BLOCKS OF SUCCESS

⭐ ⭐ ⭐ ⭐ ⭐

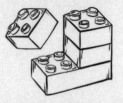

THESE 8-BOOK SET FOR TOMORROW'S LEADERS AIM TO CONVEY THE IDEA OF COMPREHENSIVE SKILL-BUILDING, PERSONAL DEVELOPMENT, AND EQUIPPING CHILDREN WITH THE TOOLS THEY NEED TO SUCCEED IN VARIOUS ASPECTS OF LIFE BEYOND ACADEMIC SUBJECTS.

FROM SAVING TO INVESTING
MONEY MATTERS FOR KIDS

EMBRACING DIFFERENCES
OUR DIVERSE WORLD

THE POWER OF SOCIAL SKILLS
BUILDING BRIDGES

NAVIGATING THE DIGITAL WORLD
TECH SAVVY

ENVIRONMENTAL STEWARDSHIP
EXPLORING OUR PLANET

UNLEASHING THE POWER OF TECHNOLOGY
CREATIVE CODING

DISCOVERING THE WONDERS OF SCIENCE
BRANCHES OF SCIENCE

EXPLORING WORLD CULTURES
GLOBAL CITIZENS

AN 8-BOOK SET FOR TOMORROW'S LEADERS.

ISBN 9798398487008

90000

9 798398 487008

I Love Fall

VONTAVIA J. HEARD